VIOLIN

All Sorts

GRADES 2–3

Selected and edited by Mary Cohen

VIOLIN PART

Faber Music in association with Trinity College London
Bloomsbury House 74–77 Great Russell Street London WC1B 3DA
fabermusic.com

PRINCE OF DENMARK'S MARCH

Imagine a grand occasion at court when you play this, with everyone
dressed in fine clothes and music provided by trumpets and drums.

Jeremiah Clarke
(c.1670–1707)

THEME FROM POLOVTSIAN DANCES

The Russian composer Borodin wrote this piece as part of a ballet scene
within his opera *Prince Igor*.

Alexander Borodin
(1833–1887)

ROBIN'S RETREAT

This piece is based on a popular sixteenth-century dance style called an allemande.
Two lines of people dance towards each other, circle around and cross to the other side.

Pam Wedgwood

FISHER LADDIE

A lot of decoration is woven around this tune, just like the
fisher laddie weaving his needle in and out as he mends the fishing nets.

Traditional (England)
unaccompanied

OUT 'N' ABOUT RAG

Music in 'ragged' time means that some beats are longer or shorter than
you might expect. The most famous ragtime composer was Scott Joplin,
who said 'you should never play them quick'.

Mary Cohen

LISON DORMAIT

This title means 'Lison was sleeping'. Imagine someone tiptoeing past in bars 9 to 16, trying not to wake Lison.

Wolfgang Amadeus Mozart
(1756–1791)

MINUET

This was originally written for the baryton – a popular instrument in Haydn's day. It had one set of strings to be plucked or bowed and another set under the fingerboard which vibrated in sympathy.

Franz Joseph Haydn
(1732–1809)

5

DANCE OF THE BLESSED SPIRITS

This is one of Gluck's best-known pieces. It comes from his opera
Orpheus and Euridice.

Christoph von Gluck
(1714–1787)

SARABANDE

Corelli was an Italian violinist and composer. Although he wrote only a few works,
his style of violin playing set new standards and influenced many composers.

Arcangelo Corelli
(1653–1713)

PADDY O'RAFFERTY

This jig would be played at a ceilidh (pronounced 'kaylee'):
an Irish or Scottish party with traditional dancing and singing.

Traditional (Irish)
unaccompanied

MARCH FROM L'ARLÉSIENNE

This tune is based on a traditional carol from Provence called *The Three Kings*.
Imagine it's being played in a procession by a pipe and drum – fading into the
distance at the end.

Georges Bizet
(1838–1875)

PAVANE

Fauré wrote this piece for a big party in Paris. The guests dressed up in
historical costumes and danced to music played by a hidden band of musicians.

Gabriel Fauré
(1845–1924)

VIOLIN

All Sorts

GRADES 2–3

Selected and edited by Mary Cohen

Piano arrangements by David Wright

PIANO ACCOMPANIMENT

Faber Music in association with Trinity College London
Bloomsbury House 74–77 Great Russell Street London WC1B 3DA
fabermusic.com

Contents

© 2003 by Faber Music Ltd and Trinity College London
First published in 2003 by Faber Music Ltd
in association with Trinity College London
Bloomsbury House 74–77 Great Russell Street London WC1B 3DA
Cover illustration by Vikki Liogier
Music processed by Jackie Leigh
Printed in England by Caligraving Ltd
All rights reserved

ISBN10: 0-571-52228-9
EAN13: 978-0-571-52228-6

To buy Faber Music or Trinity publications or to find out about the full range of titles available please contact your local music retailer or Faber Music sales enquiries:

Faber Music Ltd, Burnt Mill, Elizabeth Way, Harlow CM20 2HX
Tel: +44 (0)1279 82 89 82   Fax: +44 (0)1279 82 89 83
sales@fabermusic.com   fabermusicstore.com

PRINCE OF DENMARK'S MARCH

Imagine a grand occasion at court when you play this, with everyone
dressed in fine clothes and music provided by trumpets and drums.

Jeremiah Clarke
(c.1670–1707)

3

THEME FROM POLOVTSIAN DANCES

The Russian composer Borodin wrote this piece as part of a ballet scene
within his opera *Prince Igor.*

Alexander Borodin
(1833–1887)

ROBIN'S RETREAT

This piece is based on a popular sixteenth-century dance style called an allemande.
Two lines of people dance towards each other, circle around and cross to the other side.

Pam Wedgwood

5

OUT 'N' ABOUT RAG

Music in 'ragged' time means that some beats are longer or shorter than
you might expect. The most famous ragtime composer was Scott Joplin,
who said 'you should never play them quick'.

Mary Cohen

LISON DORMAIT

This title means 'Lison was sleeping'. Imagine someone
tiptoeing past in bars 9 to 16, trying not to wake Lison.

Wolfgang Amadeus Mozart
(1756–1791)

MINUET

This was originally written for the baryton – a popular instrument in
Haydn's day. It had one set of strings to be plucked or bowed and
another set under the fingerboard which vibrated in sympathy.

Franz Joseph Haydn
(1732–1809)

DANCE OF THE BLESSED SPIRITS

This is one of Gluck's best-known pieces. It comes from his opera
Orpheus and Euridice.

Christoph von Gluck
(1714–1787)

SARABANDE

Corelli was an Italian violinist and composer. Although he wrote only a few works,
his style of violin playing set new standards and influenced many composers.

Arcangelo Corelli
(1653–1713)

MARCH FROM L'ARLÉSIENNE

This tune is based on a traditional carol from Provence called *The Three Kings*.
Imagine it's being played in a procession by a pipe and drum – fading into the
distance at the end.

Georges Bizet
(1838–1875)

PAVANE

Fauré wrote this piece for a big party in Paris. The guests dressed up in
historical costumes and danced to music played by a hidden band of musicians.

Gabriel Fauré
(1845–1924)

GAVOTTE *from* SUITE IN D

The Bach family produced several generations of musicians, of whom
Johann Sebastian was the most famous. As well as being a great
composer, J S Bach was a virtuoso organist.

Johann Sebastian Bach
(1685–1750)

THE DEATH OF ÅSE *from* PEER GYNT SUITE

Grieg was a Norwegian composer and pianist who had a great interest in his native
folk music. Perhaps because of this, his music often contains unusual harmonies.

Edvard Grieg
(1843–1907)

16

THE BIRDS GATHER AT DUSK

When the farmers hear the birds begin to gather at dusk,
it's the signal for the end of the long working day.

Mary Cohen
after a Chinese folk song

* Harmonic

RONDO THEME *from* Op.48

Whilst a pupil of Haydn's, Pleyel wrote a piece that so impressed Haydn's
patron, that the elder musician was presented with a carriage 'for having such
a good pupil'. How fair was that?

Ignaz Pleyel
(1757–1831)

GAGLIARDO

This piece is a galliard: a dance pattern of hops and jumps. Try to reflect this
lightness when you play it and imagine the jumps in bars 4, 12, 16 and so on.

Pam Wedgwood

D.C. al Fine

LA SERENATA

Braga was an Italian cellist and composer. This piece, sometimes known as
'The Angel's Serenade', was originally written for voice and cello accompaniment.

Gaetano Braga
(1829–1907)

poco più animato

rit.

Tempo I

GAVOTTE *from* SUITE IN D

The Bach family produced several generations of musicians, of whom
Johann Sebastian was the most famous. As well as being a great
composer, J S Bach was a virtuoso organist.

Johann Sebastian Bach
(1685–1750)

Allegretto ♩ = 100

THE DEATH OF ÅSE *from* PEER GYNT SUITE

Grieg was a Norwegian composer and pianist who had a great interest in his native folk music. Perhaps because of this, his music often contains unusual harmonies.

Edvard Grieg
(1843–1907)

BIG-BROTHER BLUES

Play this jazzy tune with lots of energy and rhythmic vitality.

Pam Wedgwood
unaccompanied

10

THE BIRDS GATHER AT DUSK

When the farmers hear the birds begin to gather at dusk,
it's the signal for the end of the long working day.

Mary Cohen
after a Chinese folk song

* Harmonic

RONDO THEME *from Op.48*

Ignaz Pleyel
(1757–1831)

Whilst a pupil of Haydn's, Pleyel wrote a piece that so impressed Haydn's patron, that the elder musician was presented with a carriage 'for having such a good pupil'. How fair was that?

GAGLIARDO

Pam Wedgwood

This piece is a galliard: a dance pattern of hops and jumps. Try to reflect this lightness when you play it and imagine the jumps in bars 4, 12, 16 and so on.

STICK DANCE

This little tune is traditionally played straight and then expanded by improvisation.
A dancer waves a coloured stick decoratively in the air, drawing shapes
which follow the musical ideas.

Traditional (India)
unaccompanied

LA SERENATA

Braga was an Italian cellist and composer. This piece, sometimes known as
'The Angel's Serenade', was originally written for voice and cello accompaniment.

Gaetano Braga
(1829–1907)

rit.   Tempo I

Contents

© 2003 by Faber Music Ltd and Trinity College *London*
First published in 2003 by Faber Music Ltd
in association with Trinity College *London*
3 Queen Square London WC1N 3AU
Cover illustration by Vikki Liogier
Music processed by Jackie Leigh
Printed in England by Caligraving Ltd
All rights reserved

ISBN 0-571-52228-9

To buy Faber Music or Trinity publications or to find out about the full range of titles
available please contact your local music retailer or Faber Music sales enquiries:

Faber Music Ltd, Burnt Mill, Elizabeth Way, Harlow CM20 2HX
Tel: +44 (0)1279 82 89 82   Fax: +44 (0)1279 82 89 83
sales@fabermusic.com   fabermusic.com   trinitycollege.co.uk